The Art
Of
Money

The creative approach to mastering your finances

Brian Richson

Table of contents

Chapter One

INTRODUCTION

For many people, the idea of managing money is daunting and overwhelming. We are taught to approach money with a rigid, analytical mindset, focusing solely on numbers and figures. However, this approach can often lead to stress, anxiety and frustration and can make it difficult to achieve our financial goals.

That's where a creative approach to money comes in. By approaching money with creativity and imagination, we can change our relationship with money and make it a more positive and enjoyable experience. Creativity allows us to think outside the box, find new solutions to old problems and come up with innovative ways to manage our finances and to also break free from traditional financial thinking, creating a new approach that works for us, and to also focus on the overall purpose and meaning behind our financial goals.

In this book, we will explore the power of a creative approach to money and how it can help us achieve financial freedom and success .

Chapter Two

Why mindset matters and how to

shift it to achieve financial freedom

Money is a powerful tool that can either lead to financial freedom or financial stress. However, most people focus only on the practical aspects of money management, such as budgeting and investing, while ignoring the critical role that mindset plays in achieving financial success. In this chapter, we'll explore the importance of mindset in mastering your finances and how to shift your mindset to achieve financial freedom.

Understand the Power of Your Mindset

Your mindset refers to your attitudes, beliefs, and assumptions about money. It shapes how you think about money, how you feel about money, and how you behave around money. For example, if you believe that money is scarce, you may hoard it and feel anxious about spending it. On the other hand, if you believe money is abundant, you may be more willing to take risks and invest in yourself.

To achieve financial freedom, it's essential to understand the power of your mindset and the impact it has on your financial decisions. By recognizing your limiting beliefs and negative attitudes about money, you can start to shift your mindset towards abundance and prosperity.

Identify and Challenge Your Limiting Beliefs

The first step in shifting your mindset is to identify and challenge your limiting beliefs about money. These are the beliefs that hold you back from achieving financial success, such as "I'll never be able to save enough money" or "Money is the root of all evil." These beliefs are often deeply ingrained in our subconscious minds, and it takes effort and awareness to overcome them.

To challenge your limiting beliefs, start by questioning their validity. Ask yourself, "Is this belief really true? Where did it come from? What evidence do I have to support it?" Then, replace your limiting beliefs with positive affirmations, such as "I am worthy of financial abundance" or "Money flows easily and freely to me."

Cultivate an Abundance Mindset

To shift your mindset towards financial freedom, it's important to cultivate an abundance mindset. This means focusing on the abundance and prosperity that already exists in your life, rather than on what you lack. Practice gratitude for what you have, and focus on the possibilities and opportunities that exist for you.

Visualize Your Financial Freedom

Visualize yourself achieving your financial goals and living a life of financial freedom. See yourself with a healthy bank account, traveling the world, or pursuing your passions. This visualization helps you stay motivated and focused on your goals, and trains your mind to see financial freedom as a reality.

Develop Positive Habits and Practices

Start by creating a budget and tracking your expenses, so you have a clear understanding of where your money is going. Set financial goals and create a plan for achieving them. Automate your savings and investments, so you don't have to rely on willpower to save money.

Practice self-discipline and delayed gratification by avoiding impulsive purchases and focusing on long-term goals. Develop a growth mindset by committing to ongoing learning and education about personal finance. Surround yourself with people who support your financial goals and encourage your growth.

Celebrate Your Financial Wins

No matter how small they may seem, recognize your progress and give yourself credit for the hard work and effort you're putting in. Celebrating your wins helps reinforce positive habits and practices, boosts your confidence, and keeps you motivated to continue on your path to financial freedom.

Learn from your mistakes

We all make mistakes with our money, but the key is to learn from those mistakes and use them as opportunities for growth and not beating up ourselves over past mistakes.

Surround yourself with positive influences

The People you surround yourself with have in one way or another an impact on your ability to achieve success. It is important to keep people who push and motivate you, and people who also have a growth mindset not just with money but with other things in life.

Chapter Three

Your money story: uncovering and rewriting your money story for financial success

Have you ever stopped to think about your money story? I mean, it's the story you've been telling yourself about money for years now. It's based on your experiences, upbringing, cultural background, and societal messages you've been exposed to. And let me tell you, it can have a significant impact on your finances!

So, let's dive in and uncover your money story. Start by asking yourself some questions. What did you learn about money growing up? How do you feel about money currently? Do you believe that money is scarce or abundant? How do you view wealth and success?

It's helpful to write down your thoughts and feelings about money in a journal. Take a moment to reflect on where these beliefs may have come from. But keep in mind, don't judge yourself or your experiences.

Now, let's examine whether your current money story is helping or hindering your financial success. For example, if you believe that money is scarce and hard to come by, you might experience anxiety and stress around finances, which can lead to overspending or undersaving. However, if you believe that money is abundant and flowing, you may be more open to opportunities for financial growth and abundance.

But, here's the exciting part. You have the power to rewrite your money story! Once you've identified the beliefs and attitudes that are holding you back, you can intentionally shift your mindset towards a more abundant and positive outlook on money.

One great way to do this is by creating affirmations that align with your desired financial reality. Affirmations are positive statements that you repeat to yourself to reinforce new beliefs and behaviors. For example, if you want to cultivate a more abundant mindset, you could create affirmations like:

I am open to receiving abundance and

wealth in my life.

Money flows easily and effortlessly to

me.

I trust in my ability to create financial

success and abundance.

Visualization exercises are another great way to help you manifest your desired financial reality. Take some time each day to visualize yourself achieving your financial goals, feeling confident and empowered around money, and enjoying a sense of financial freedom and security.

Rewriting your money story takes time and patience, but with commitment and practice, you can create a new financial reality that aligns with your goals and values.

Chapter four

How to create a budget that works

for you

Budgeting is a crucial skill to master when it comes to managing your finances, but it's often seen as a boring and tedious task. However, what if I told you that creating a budget can be a creative process that empowers you to take control of your finances and live the life you want? In this chapter, I'll show you how to make budgeting an art form that works for you.

First things first, let's start with your financial goals. What do you want to achieve? Whether it's paying off debt, saving for a down payment on a house, or taking a dream vacation, write them down and prioritize them. Knowing your goals will help you create a budget that aligns with them.

Next, track your income and expenses. This may seem daunting, but it's easier than you think. You can use a spreadsheet, a budgeting app, or even just a pen and paper to track your money. Be sure to include all sources of income and all of your expenses. This will help you identify where your money is going and where you can make changes.

Now, categorize your expenses. This could include categories like housing, transportation, food, entertainment, and more. Categorizing your expenses will help you see where you're spending the most money and where you might be able to cut back.

Based on your financial goals and your expenses, set spending limits for each category. This will help you stay on track and avoid overspending. But don't forget to leave some wiggle room for unexpected expenses.

But just remember, your budget isn't set in stone. Review it regularly and adjust it as needed. Maybe you need to increase your spending in one category or cut back in another. Be flexible and make changes when necessary.

Get creative! You know, budgeting doesn't have to be a boring and restrictive task like we envision it to be. You can always find ways to make it fun and enjoyable. It could be a   challenge to yourself to find ways to save money each month, or you create a vision board of your financial goals. Whatever it is, make budgeting a positive and empowering experience.

Creating a budget that works for you is an art form, one that takes time and effort to master.

Budgeting isn't restrictive or limiting – it's liberating.

Chapter five

How to generate multiple streams

of income

As someone who has struggled with finances in the past, I know firsthand the feeling of being stuck in a financial rut with just one source of income. I used to rely solely on my 9-to-5 job and felt like I was barely making ends meet. It wasn't until I started exploring creative income streams that I was able to gain financial stability and freedom.

Luckily, you and I are going to explore some creative income streams which you might not have considered before.

Freelancing:
 Freelancing is a great way to earn income doing something you love. Essentially, freelancing means that you're providing a service to clients on a project-by-project basis. It's a great option for people who want to work on their own terms and be their own boss. As a freelancer, you can set your own rates, choose the projects you work on, and decide when and where you work. For example, let's say you're a graphic designer. You could offer your services to clients on websites like Upwork or Fiverr. You could also reach out to potential clients directly, either

through social media or networking events. By building a strong reputation and delivering high-quality work, you can build long-term relationships with clients and grow your income over time.

Online Courses:
Online courses are a great way to share your expertise with others and earn passive income. Essentially, you're creating a digital product that people can purchase and access at any time. Online courses can cover a wide range of topics, from cooking to photography to business.
Creating a successful online course requires a few key steps. First, you need to identify a specific problem or need that your course will solve. Then, you need to create content that

provides value to your students and is engaging and easy to follow. Finally, you need to market your course effectively to reach your target audience.

For example, let's say you're an expert in yoga. You could create an online course that teaches people how to practice yoga at home. You could include video lessons, written guides, and a community forum for students to connect with each other. By pricing your course appropriately and marketing it effectively, you can generate passive income while sharing your knowledge with others.

Affiliate Marketing:
Affiliate marketing is a great way to earn passive income by promoting

someone else's product or service. Essentially, you're earning a commission for every sale that comes from your referral link.

To be successful at affiliate marketing, it's important to choose products or services that align with your brand and that you genuinely believe in. It's also important to disclose your affiliate relationships to your audience, so they understand that you're receiving a commission for any sales that come from your link.

Let's say you're a beauty blogger. You could partner with a makeup brand and promote their products to your audience. You could create makeup tutorials using their products, write reviews of their products, and include your affiliate link in your blog posts. By providing value to your audience and promoting products that you believe in, you can generate passive income through affiliate marketing.

Rental Income:
 Rental income is a great way to earn passive income by renting out property that you own. This can include residential properties, commercial properties, or vacation rentals.
To be successful at rental income, it's important to have a solid understanding of the real estate market and property management. You'll need to find the right properties to invest in, price your rentals appropriately, and manage your tenants effectively. Rental income can be a great source of passive income,

but it does require some upfront investment and ongoing management. For example, let's say you own a vacation rental property in a popular tourist destination. You could rent out your property through Airbnb or VRBO and generate passive income throughout the year. By providing a great experience for your guests and managing your property effectively, you can earn a steady stream of rental income.

Investing:
Investing is a great way to grow your wealth over time and generate passive income through dividends, interest, or capital gains. There are many different types of investments, including stocks, bonds, real estate, and more.

To be successful at investing, it's important to have a solid understanding of the financial markets and to have a long-term investment strategy. You'll need to research different investment options, diversify your portfolio, and monitor your investments regularly. While investing can be a great source of passive income, it does carry some risk and requires careful management. Now , let's say you invest in stocks through a brokerage account. By purchasing dividend-paying stocks and holding them for the long term, you can earn passive income through regular dividend payments. Over time, your investments may also grow in value, allowing you to generate passive income through capital gains.

Royalties:
 Royalties are a great way to earn passive income if you have creative work that you own, such as music, books, or artwork. Essentially, royalties are payments that you receive for the use of your creative work.
To earn royalties, you'll need to create something that is valuable to others and that can be used or licensed by others. For example, if you're a musician, you could create original music and license it for use in TV shows, movies, or commercials. By earning royalties on your creative work, you can generate passive income over time.

E-commerce:
E-commerce is a great way to earn income by selling products online. This

can include physical products, digital products, or services.

To be successful at e-commerce, you need to identify a niche market and create products that meet the needs of that market. You'll need to create an online store, market your products effectively, and manage your inventory and shipping. While e-commerce can be a great source of income, it does require some upfront investment and ongoing management.

If you're a jewelry designer. You could create an online store and sell your jewelry to customers all over the world. By creating unique and high-quality products, marketing your brand effectively, and providing excellent customer service, you can generate income through e-commerce.

Real Estate Flipping:
Real estate flipping is a great way to earn income by buying and renovating properties for a profit. Essentially, you're buying properties that need work, making improvements to the properties, and then selling them for a profit.

And if you want to be successful at real estate flipping, you need to have a solid understanding of the real estate market and property renovations. You'll need to find properties that are undervalued or in need of repair, make improvements that add value to the property, and then sell the property at a profit. While real estate flipping can be a great source of income, it does carry some risk and requires careful management.

Chapter six

The joy of saving

One of the best ways to make saving money a fun and rewarding experience is to set goals and celebrate milestones. Setting goals gives you something tangible to work towards and breaking them down into smaller milestones can help you stay motivated along the way. Celebrating milestones can also create a sense of accomplishment and positive reinforcement that encourages you to keep going.

Challenge your friends and family to a savings competition, track your progress, and reward the winner.

You could also automate your savings, Set up automatic transfers from your checking account to your savings account, and watch your savings grow without even trying. It's like magic!

Try not to think of saving as a drag, try to think of it as an opportunity. Picture yourself on a sandy beach in your dream destination, or sipping a latte in your new home.

And of course, you should never forget to enjoy life along the way. Treat yourself to a small reward when you reach milestones or achieve your goals. A nice dinner or a new pair of shoes can go a long way in making the journey more enjoyable.

Try a no-spend challenge: Challenge yourself to a week or even a month where you don't spend any money on non-essential items. It's a great way to reset your spending habits and can help you save a significant amount of money.

Join a savings challenge online: There are many online savings challenges that you can join, such as the 52-week money challenge, where you save a small amount each week that gradually increases over the year. You can also find savings challenges on social media or by creating your own with friends.

Chapter seven

Creative debt reduction

Debt can feel like a weight on your shoulders, dragging you down and making it hard to get ahead financially. But it doesn't have to be that way. By taking a creative approach to debt reduction, you can pay off your debt and start building wealth for the future.

Here are some strategies to help you: do just that:

Create a budget:

 A budget is like a road map for your money, and it's important to have one so you don't end up lost and broke in the middle of nowhere. Plus, it's a great opportunity to flex your math skills and feel like a financial wizard. Who needs Hogwarts when you have spreadsheets, am I right?

Track your expenses:

Keeping track of your expenses is like being a detective for your own wallet.

You get to hunt down every penny you've spent and figure out where it's all going. And who knows, maybe you'll uncover some shocking truths – like how much money you've spent on impulse buys at the grocery store.

Cut back on unnecessary expenses:

Cutting back on expenses can be tough, but it's all about making sacrifices for the greater good. And hey, maybe you'll find some creative ways to save money – like using your gym membership to hang your laundry instead of paying for a dryer. Okay, maybe that's a bit extreme, but you get the idea.

Increase your income:
They say money can't buy happiness, but it sure can buy a lot of things that make us happy. That's why it's important to find ways to increase your income. And who knows, maybe your new side hustle will allow you to finally buy that hot tub you've been eyeing.

Negotiate with creditors:

Negotiating with creditors can be a bit intimidating, but it's all about playing hardball – or maybe just softball, depending on your negotiation skills. Just remember to bring your A-game and your best puppy dog eyes. Who can say no to someone with puppy dog eyes?

Consider debt consolidation:

Debt consolidation is like a superhero that swoops in to save the day – or in this case, your bank account. It can simplify your payments and make your debt more manageable, like a spa day for your finances. Who doesn't love a good financial spa day?

Epilogue

In a world where money is often viewed as a source of stress and anxiety, "The Art of Money" offers a refreshing perspective on how to approach our finances. Through its creative and holistic approach, this book empowers readers to transform their relationship with money and unlock a new found sense of financial freedom. Whether you're an artist, entrepreneur, or simply someone looking to take control of your finances, "The Art of Money" is a must-read guidebook that will inspire and motivate you to achieve your financial goals with creativity and joy. So go ahead, embrace your inner artist and let "The Art of Money" guide you on your journey to financial mastery.